HardcoreRap

Hardcore Rap

A Fusion of Metal, Rock, and Hip-Hop

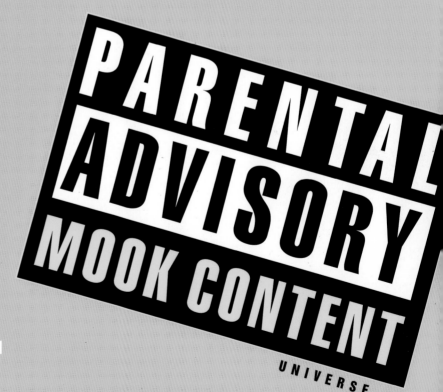

PARENTAL ADVISORY

MOOK CONTENT

UNIVERSE

Arion Berger

First published in the United States of America in 2001
by UNIVERSE PUBLISHING
A Division of Rizzoli International Publications, Inc.
300 Park Avenue South
New York, NY 10010

© 2001 Universe Publishing

 2001 2002 2003 2004 2005 / 10 9 8 7 6 5 4 3 2 1

Printed in Hong Kong

Library of Congress Catalog Card Number: 00-111822

ardcoreRapContents

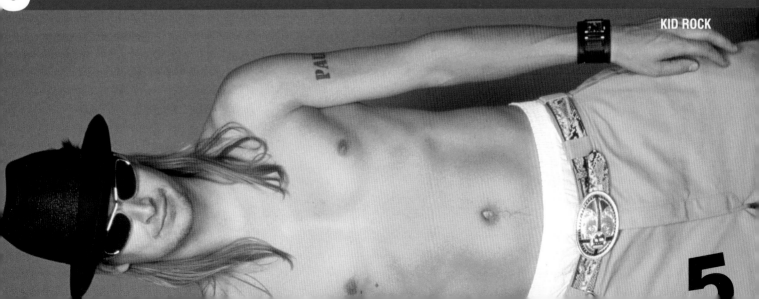

KID ROCK

LIMP BIZKIT

WHATA

Mooks aren't new. They've always been with us, under different aliases. Varmint, knave, greaser, gangsta, head-banger, slacker, punk, pimp, juvenile delinquent, screw-up, superstar. You know who you are. The look might change, but the attitude remains the same.

LOOK!

8

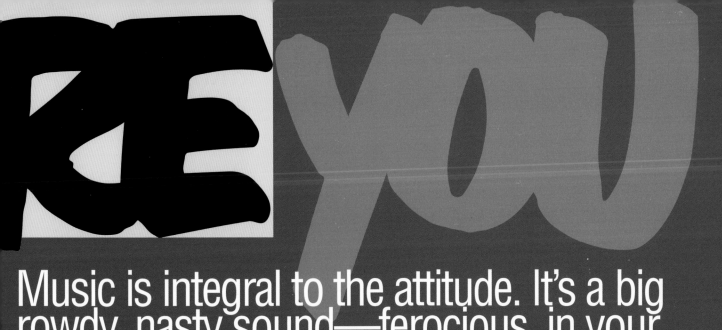

RE YOU

Music is integral to the attitude. It's a big rowdy, nasty sound—ferocious, in your face, brutally honest: It looks under the rocks most people don't want to touch. And eventually, you have to give everything up to that sound, a monstrous thumping beat that seems to come from

NGAT?

9

inside your own body and makes your head bang back and forth, beyond your control.

Now we call the sound metal-rap, or rapcore, or hip-rock, or gangsta thrash, but all the names mean one thing: this is music by, for, and about the young, angry, and imaginative. Regardless of race or color, gender or religion, it's an elite democracy of the thoroughly pissed-off. It is not for everyone.

This is a celebration of the young and rowdy, the loud and snotty, the furious bands and masta pimps that have made mookdom a badge of honor and the sound of the century. **Let's break stuff.**

People Who Will Never Be Mooks

1 Anyone who asks if your piercings, tattoos, broken collarbone, or two-timing girlfriend hurt you.

2 Anyone whose idea of "lifestyle" means coordinating their household accessories.

3 Anyone who's seen Riverdance live will never be a mook.

4 You used to play Dungeons & Dragons? It's cool. Just don't advertise it, okay?

5 That chicken-necked geek who hangs around your homeboys. Wants to know what "chronic" means. No way.

6 Anyone in the 4-H Club. No farmer will ever be a mook. He's too freaking busy.

7 Anyone who claims to see people's auras is never gonna get close to being a mook.

LIT

11

SHOUT

What was rapcore before it stomped all over the airwaves and made teen pop queens cry? In the dark ages of the '80s, there was rap and there was hardcore. Both styles were music for outcasts. Politicians thought rap was dangerous and critics wouldn't touch anything that had the word "core" in it.

The Red Hot Chili Peppers reveal why they're called the Fathers of Metal Rap.

Beastie Boys dream of a future when they can each have their own slice of pizza.

Licensed To Ill
remains perma-
nently listed in
the Billboard
Top Pop Catalog
Albums chart. It's
still one of the
most-purchased
albums in the U.S.

17

Anthony Kiedis of the RED HOT CHILI PEPPERS

But there were stirrings. Urban white kids were experimenting with the music that spoke loudest to them.

New York's snottiest punk-rock trio the Beastie Boys had been a lousy, unsuccessful punk band in the early '80s, but after blasting onto the hip-hop scene with *Licensed To Ill* (1989), they opened up the floodgates for clever white-guy rap, Brooklyn-bound, and hard at the core despite the fact that members weren't exactly raised in the projects. The Beastie Boys even went back to playing instruments behind its sneering, supersmart rap on *Check Your Head* (1992).

Over in sunny Southern California, the Red Hot Chili Peppers were recovering from being a polished, kind of pretentious, hard-rock/art band in high school. Bassist Flea's fascination with funk and the hiring of high-school pal Anthony Keidis as lead singer expanded their sound into fresh territory. In 1985 the Peppers drafted funkmeister George Clinton to produce their cult breakthrough *Freaky Styley*. But it wasn't until 1991, when rap impresario Rick Rubin signed on to mastermind *Blood Sugar Sex Magik*, that the Peppers perfected its sound—a mix of pounding hip-hop and thrash

KID ROCK,
AEROSMITH,
RUN-DMC at
1999 MTV
Video Music
Awards, NYC

Now point to the man who started it all. Now sweat. Good work, Ice-T.

21

Hard-drinking, hard-rocking Irish boys with ghetto envy, HOUSE OF PAIN had a rap 'n' roll smash with "Jump Around."

speed (part of it imported by Flea from his stint with legendary punk band Fear).

Around the same time, a thick, slow cloud of intoxicating smoke was hovering over a very small section of Los Angeles. Under this cloud could be found Cypress Hill, a trio of pro-weed two Latino guys and an Italian-American who were as politically active as they were musically groundbreaking. When they burst onto the scene in the early '90s, no one else was making the same sound—a mix of ambient techno adapted from the English aural wallpaper style called trip-hop—looping burnout beats thundering from the rhythm section, and rapper B-Real's distinctive snotty vocals. Cypress Hill sounded slow and dangerous, like a steamroller bearing down on the listener's ass, and their staunch stance on marijuana legalization made them as famous as their music.

It wasn't just white and Latino kids adapting hip-hop style; there was also a move within the rap community to tap the big, loyal metal audience. After all, even if politicians and critics didn't get it—the attitude, the sense of power-lessness, and the fury of the metal were the same as rap's—why shouldn't the audience cross over? The first rap star to make a move was Original Gangster Ice-T, the hip-hop power-house who joined the first Lollapalooza tour in 1991 at the request of Perry Farrell, founder of the festival revival and Los Angeles's legendary screaming art-metal outfit Jane's Addiction. A smart businessman and brilliant reader of the cultural temperature, Ice-T saw the same mad, messy kids shrieking along to his dark 'hood scenarios as were headbanging to Metallica. In 1991 he assembled Body Count, a nihilistic hardcore band featuring the O.G. himself on

23

Run-DMC were already hip-hop veterans when they showed '70's rockers Aerosmith a new way to sing about chicks.

25

vocals. The political mood was tense, and politicians too

protective of their salaries to protect the First Amendment and the benefits of an intellectually diverse society called for a precedent-setting ban on Body Count's self-explanatory single, "Cop Killer."

Ice-T had the nerve to propose that angry, disenfranchised urban youths of all colors resent the bullying tactics of a powerful and untouchable police system. And everyone went berserk. Parents groups and censorship forces thought they had found the Holy Grail of Music That Should Be Banned. The NRA seemed to forget that it was all about the guns and protested the song's existence, as did police activist groups. Ice-T's label, Warner Brothers, claimed to support its artist's right to free speech but wouldn't release his next album *Home Invasion*, because they objected to the cover.

It took a soft touch to bring the two styles—and the not-very-disparate worlds of "black" and "white" music—to the mainstream masses. Lite metal and old-school party rap stalked the stage and shot up the charts. It made number 4 in 1986 when Run-D.M.C. teamed up with '70's power-rockers Aerosmith for a blistering new version of Aerosmith's "Walk This Way." In 1991 rock returned the favor when Anthrax, a thrash-metal group already showing nervy hip-hop tendencies, amped up Public Enemy's call to power "Bring Tha Noize." Soon after, House of Pain, a trio of thuggish Irish goofballs scored number 3 on the pop charts with a big-beat party anthem, "Jump Around," full of weird whistles and bellowing background shouts. It's no surprise that House of Pain made a crossover splash. Before creating the group, essential member Everlast

"Now I'm black, but black people trip because white people like me and they don't like them."
—ICE-T, Race War

27

What do you
mean we've got
Anthrax? Oh, we
ARE Anthrax.

29

Poor VANILLA ICE was clueless, on top of everything else, although the brothers can obviously smell the impending doom.

had been a solo rapper and a member of Ice-T's Rhyme Syndicate, a loose aggregation of friends, followers, and fellow musicians, many of them signed to Ice's label of the same name.

This section would not be complete without mention of a rap-metal pioneer who scored a number one single and album, ruled MTV's heavy rotation schedule, starred in his own vanity-project film, and set the style for a generation of screaming teenyboppers who might never have listened to rap if it weren't for him. Unfortunately, this person is Vanilla Ice. But a little perspective here—"Ice Ice Baby" wasn't the hardest hip-hop on the waves, but the deep pulsating of the Queen/David Bowie project "Under Pressure" that rolled beneath it did bring together not just rap and metal, but hip-hop-lite and arty progressive-bombast rock. The lyrics were nonsensical (What was he talking about, anyway?), but the beat was undeniable, and no one else had thought of it. It's going through your head now, isn't it? You're nodding a little along with the beat, right? Yeah, we rest our case.

These bands and collaborations helped rede-fine "crossover"—which used to mean tradition-ally "black" music finding a large white pop audi-ence—as the place where attitude and style meet, regardless of race. We salute the pioneers and proto-mooks—and yes, you, Vanilla, now back in your box!—and the ball of aggression they got rolling back in the day.

MOOKS

The undisputed current kings of metal-rap are five boys from Jacksonville, Florida, we like to call **Limp Bizkit**. In the face of so many imitators and second-string wannabes, in a world in which the fusion of metal and rap is becoming a hopeless cliché, Bizkit manages to attract huge crowds at its legendary live shows. Its records outsell those of all

TODAY

competitors, and no matter how big they become, how high-rollin' the boys get, they always manage to hang onto the most precious and intangible property—its street cred.

Whatever the rapcore rules are, Limp Bizkit breaks them. The members of Limp Bizkit single-handedly turned nasty into nice and vice-versa, "decorating" their stages with giant toilets and greeting their fans and each other with the handy one-finger salute.

The members of Limp Bizkit became rock stars the old-fashioned way, by touring incessantly, hauling their own equipment, and playing everywhere they could. For four years, word-of-mouth carried the gospel of Limp Bizkit, and over that time its audience, and its reputation, grew. After appearing amid the thongs and sandals of the MTV Spring Break '98 Fashion Show, Bizkit was offered a big-time slot on the Family Values Tour of that same summer.

It also helped to have cool friends. After Korn bassist Fieldy got some tattoos from Fred Durst (he did skin art by day), Korn handed Bizkit's demo tape to their own producer. Eventually, "Nookie," from *Significant Other*, blew Bizkit onto the top of the charts. The single's MTV exposure meant that high-school freshmen across the country started chopping their baggy jeans and growing soul patches. Eventually, Fred became an industry suit himself when Interscope Records offered to make him senior vice president. Despite stiff competition from pals, colleagues, and imitators, Bizkit's reign continues—nobody, but nobody, puts on a live show with the monster aggro and unstable nitroglycerine energy that Fred & Co. unleash onstage. Soon, we hope, Fred will be able to buy himself a new red baseball cap.

Kid Rock also had a tough hill to climb. It

"Like when I come up with a really good rhyme or a good cadence I feel like Shakespeare. Or Shakes the Clown."
—Princess Superstar

The title song from Limp Bizkit's *Chocolate Starfish and the Hot-Dog Flavored Water* contains the word "fuck" more than 50 times.

Yesterday's News	Five Minutes Ago	Now
Malt liquor	Caffeinated water	Pickle juice
Getting caught carrying marijuana in an airport	Having blunts FedExed to your hotel room	Running a legal hemp farm
Lollapalooza	Woodstock '99	Ozzfest
Wanna come backstage and meet the band?	Wanna come up to my room and hear my new song?	Show us yer tits!

37

10 Ways to Know You're a Mook

1 If you knew what you were angry at, you wouldn't be so f—ing angry.

2 Who wears short shorts. Losers, that's who.

3 That thing you did, the one you wish everyone would forget— your friends turned it into a nickname.

4 You've worn dreads and scraggly chin fuzz, but never at the same time.

5 Your girlfriend's stage name is Porsche. It's also her real name.

6 You can fling your hands out in a menacing fashion while stalking around the stage, well, the basement, in a full crouch.

7 Beer: It's not just for breakfast anymore.

8 WWOD. What Would Ozzy Do?

9 You can't decide between the flaming devil's head with his tongue sticking out or a tasteful "Thug 4 Life" tattoo.

10 The Southern Baptist Convention doesn't want you for a member.

"There's a million of us just like me, who cuss like me, who just don't give a f—k like me, who dress like me, walk, talk and act like me."

The real Slim Shady? **Eminem,** aka Marshall Mathers III, made mainstream mayhem with his ultraviolent fantasies and monster beats. Brilliant, hilarious, and undeniably evil—no wonder he needs an alias.

39

STUCK MOJO's side project *Fozzy*, an album of heavy-metal cover songs, will team Mojo members with wrestler Chris Jericho.

311

41

In November 2000, Nora Garza, the features editor at the McAllen, TX *Monitor*, was fired for running this photo. THE DEFTONES sent Garza money to help pay her bills, as did the owner of FUCT, an L.A.-based clothing company.

42

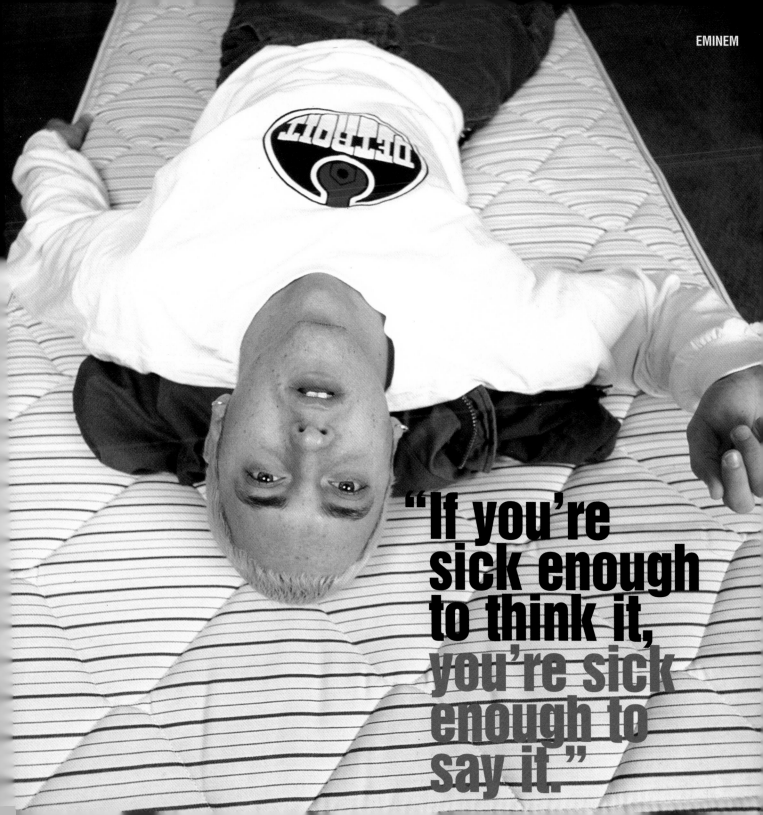

"If you're sick enough to think it, you're sick enough to say it."

wasn't until his fourth album that Kid's distinctive brand of shirtless shit-kicking hick-hop caught fire. Up until *Devil Without a Cause*, Kid had been a joke—a white-boy tagalong—in the blasted wasteland around Detroit. He was a lanky pale-face breakdancer and rap fanatic when the Beastie Boys sound opened his nose to the possibilities of hardcore folded into the rowdy rap mix. He was signed to Jive Records, but the label wasn't impressed with Kid's Beastie Boys copycat sound on his debut, *Grits Sandwiches for Breakfast*, and they dumped him. Then he signed with the Continuum label, where another record, weirdly called *The Polyfuze Method*, also bombed, the victim of mixed reviews and Kid's lack of focus.

Down but not out, Kid went back to paying for his own studio time, making *Early Mornin' Stoned Pimp* in 1996, and selling bootleg dubs of this and other albums from the back of a truck. Despite the hard times, Kid Rock managed to assemble a band of crazy local boys, including the late rapper and superfan Joe C. Finally, Atlantic Records took a chance on this pimpin' white-trash "cowboy," and the rest is rapcore history. Except for the fronters complaining about Kid's "overnight success," that is.

The crossover from rap to metal usually goes one way—white kids get interested in hip-hop and bring urban sound and attitude into the suburbs. But some performers cross racial lines in the other direction. The Latino and Italian homeboys of Cypress Hill began kickin' funky rock elements into the rap mix as early as 1988. Since then, many other outfits have followed their lead: New Kingdom's Nosaj sports a massive Afro, and his partner-in-crime Sebastian brings hardcore punk know-how to their revolutionary metal-rap

44

Kid Rock is the only metal-rap star who has a deal with a toy company to produce his own action figure, complete with red fedora.

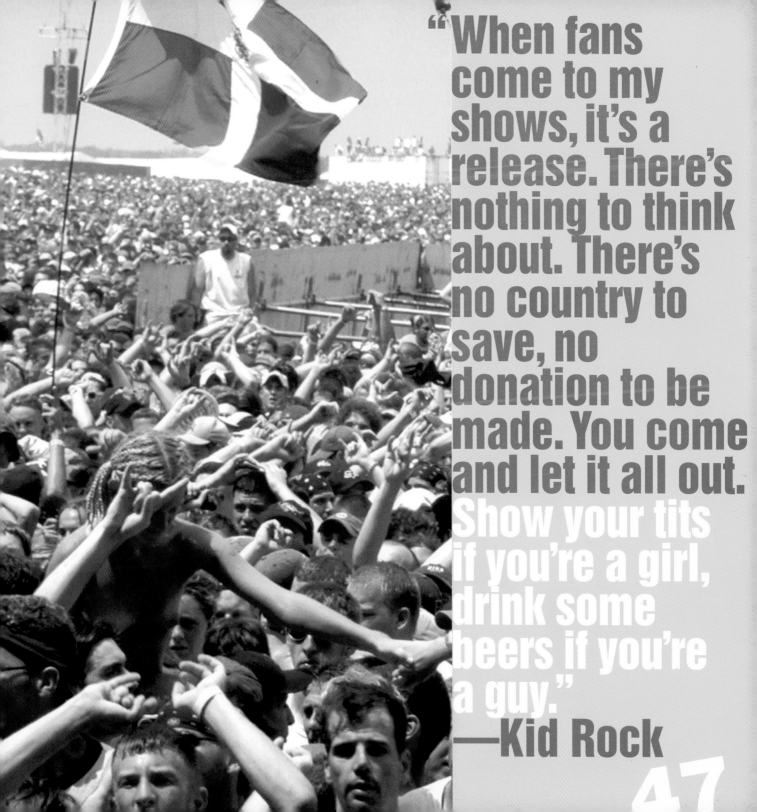

"When fans come to my shows, it's a release. There's nothing to think about. There's no country to save, no donation to be made. You come and let it all out. Show your tits if you're a girl, drink some beers if you're a guy."
—Kid Rock

47

48

1 Insane Clown Posse's Violent J dressed as a giant pizza and waved at cars for ten bucks a day.

2 Jonathan Davis from Korn was a mortuary science student.

3 Limp Bizkit's Sam Rivers worked at Chick-Fil-A.

4 His cousin John Otto played tuba in high school.

5 Wes Borland's high-school nickname was Freak.

6 Eminem was a cook at Gilbert's Lodge, a Michigan family restaurant. (He was fired five days before Christmas and then wrote "Rock Bottom.")

7 Beastie Boy's Adam Rauch rented boats at the boathouse in Central Park.

49

sound. And Atlanta's Stuck Mojo looks like any other mook on the rampage, except for African-American frontman Bonz, whose presence kept the Mojos out of the VIP room of stardom thanks to, um, Southern attitudes. Shootyz Groove, one of the hardest, most serious and all-about-the-music bands out there, has two MC's (Sense and Season) as well as a booming rhythm section of bass and drums.

Insane Clown Posse also started out as a hip-hop outfit, a consortium of Detroit hardasses calling themselves Inner City Posse. After the band combusted, a couple of Joes left behind—childhood friends Joseph Bruce and Joseph Ustler—renamed themselves Violent J and Shaggy 2 Dope and revved up the psychotronic carnival ride that is the current ICP. After numerous Joker Cards (that's what J and Shaggy call their records) and years of shaking the cages of its Faygo-guzzling loyal followers, the Juggalos, ICP has never compromised, never released a "clean" version of any single—oh, yeah, never released any singles—and never subverted their taste for psychopathic showbiz in the name of holy gold and 'NSync-size record sales.

The blonde bombshell who goes by the name Princess Superstar may be metal-rap royalty now, but as Concetta Kirshner she was pure hip-hop, a prankster bitch with a string of rude jokes, a couple of tape decks, and spiderweb wordplay that sticks to its victim. As Princess, though, her punk-rock roots started to show, and fans and critics hailed her as a blindingly smart wordsmith and ace beat manipulator.

But most rapcore stars have roots in hard rock, punk rock, or alternative. Half of Orange 9mm (singer Chaka Malik and guitarist Christ Traynor) used to be half of Burn, a hardcore punk

52

"Stoned pimp freak, stoned out of my mind / I once was lost but now I'm just blind." —Kid Rock

outfit. They rappified themselves after forming 9mm in the early '90s and spent most of the decade touring and playing, with a revolving door for various band members, and putting out only three full-length records.

You have to look back more than a dozen years to find the first generation of genuine metal-rap gods that stampeded over the barriers broken down by the forefathers. Brooklyn's Biohazard got together in 1988, the members channeled their urban frustration and youthful resentment into a churning thrash sound that got them tour dates with other politically conscious bands. In the early '90s Biohazard began to incorporate hip-hop into its earbleed metal, collaborating with rappers Onyx and perfecting its metal-rap fusion as well as its apocalyptic live show.

The rock world—punk, hardcore, and alternative—opened up a new world for SoCal's System of a Down. It started out playing a tight, melodic metal-rap groove, but overhauled it with a thrash-Goth infusion. Both P.O.D. and 311 work with twisty Latin rhythms and ungangstalike positivity. And Blindside, a Swedish rapcore group, plays a kind of rap-fueled Christian heavy metal more common to the European scene than the usually godless U.S. one.

Like multitudes of Orange County, California, roughnecks, Zebrahead dabbled in thrash and ska-punk, before jettisoning the straight-metal thing and hiring Ali Tabatabaee as chief rapper and mischief maker. While up north in the Golden State, the Deftones knelt to no one. Its jet-propelled metal has all the insistence of rap and all the melodicism of pop, and owes little to its predecessors. Once the imitators get tired of playing mook dressup, bands like the Deftones will be driving the form into the future.

"Your government will not make cannabis legal because they can't actually sell it to you."
—Serj of SYSTEM OF A DOWN

THE LO

When you're a mook, having style means never wearing a white dress shirt. It's the look that screams, "I'm not like you and I don't want what you want." You can see it on the school-yard and the streets, in cities where record deals are being made, in sub-urban garages where the undiscovered are kickin' it and the neighbors are screaming, "Turn that noise down!" The look is not sold together in stores.

SYSTEM OF A DOWN

57

Welcome to our nightmare, suckahs!

58

59

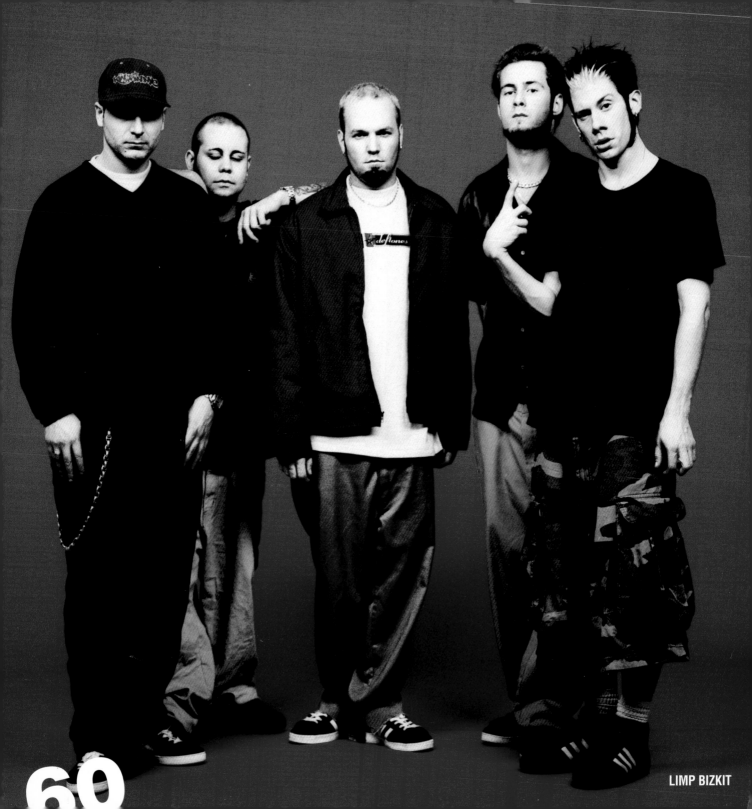

60

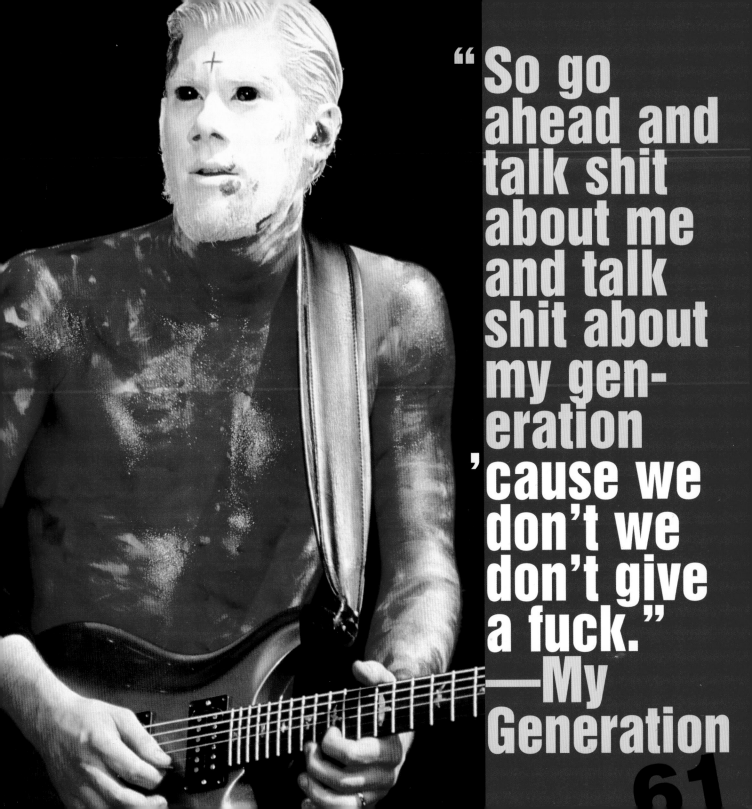

"So go ahead and talk shit about me and talk shit about my generation 'cause we don't we don't give a fuck."
—My Generation

61

James "Munky" Shaffer of Korn is missing the top third of his left index finger.

In a time when all pop music sounds alike and every wannabe star puts on the same pair of Brady Bunch pants, metal-rap is sporting the most insane knife-edge style in the business. It doesn't take a genius to figure out the roots of the look—prison-yard gangsta cred. and rock 'n' roll aggro—but there are as many variations as there are flavors of Faygo. Just look at Limp Bizkit's Wes Borland, who doesn't let being in a workaday, every-guy mook band stop him from dressing like a Goth-glam nightmare on an acid bender. He's got a different insane-in-the-brain disguise for every tour, sometimes every show, from dancing skeleton to red body paint to ...creepy unidentified ...thing.

Rock means reinvention, and most enterprising stars find their own style in spite of their background, making humble into homie, geek

RED HOT CHILI PEPPER's Dave Navarro rocks the runway.

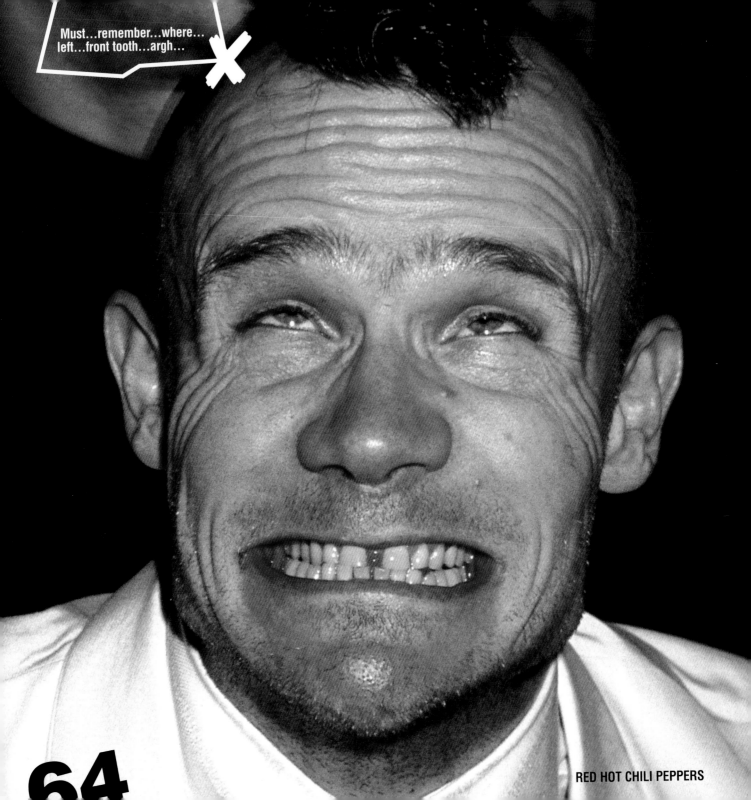

Must...remember...where...
left...front tooth...argh...

64

RED HOT CHILI PEPPERS

65

66

D-Nice and Clark Kent explain to Kid Rock why his hair choice is just so wrong.

67

into glitter. Kid Rock musta' never gotten over being from a place called Romeo. If the suffocating Michigan town gave him nothing else, it gave him the inspiration to do two things: become Romeo himself, and get the hell out. Now Rock's the worldwide masta pimp goofing on the ladies' man look, swinging wide in big floppy fedoras and the largest-livin', in-your-face fur coats. And no shirt, because, face it, with all that flash gear, a man doesn't need anything touching his chest except one of his hard honeys.

Rock's Pimp of da Nation style might be a hick update of another blond superstar and Music City homeboy—Vanilla Ice. Ice also had long hair (although it went forward instead of back, like Kid Rock's 'do), and his ridiculous stars-and-stripes sweatsuits were a nod in the direction of Run-DMC comfortwear made boxing-ring-ready for the likes of Apollo Creed or similar pathetic tomato cans.

Fred Durst never tried to dress for success, but opportunity knocked anyway. Then again, it wasn't a sharp blue suit that made the power-boys at Interscope Records offer Fred Durst a position as senior vice president—it was his ears. They figured that if he can turn five pissed-off Florida kids with a weird name into a rock phenomenon, he could tap other struggling bands for a recording contract and make Interscope—and the Limp Bizkit Corporation, all profits to be divided by F. Durst, CEO—enough bizkit dough to feed your whole family reunion including your greedy Auntie Mae. His style is all street and no compromise, from the pointy chin fuzz to the gallery's-worth of tattoos, the clothes—baggy long shorts, band T-shirts, and bouncy sneakers—built for maximum action onstage.

68

BIOHAZARD

69

Dressed only in socks or plugged into sock- ets, Red Hot Chili Peppers didn't call one record **Freaky Styley for**

72

BIOHAZARD—
stand back. Ink
poisoning area.

Mooks need to be comfortable—it's the attitude that makes a statement, not the threads. Rage Against the Machine set the no-look look standard. The members of Rage had no time to be primping so long as the world continued on its messed-up course. Jeans and T-shirts—you got a problem with that? Bands from Los Angeles to the Bronx inherited the regular-guy style, with Shootyz Groove bundling up for harsh New York winters in flannel, windbreakers, and knit caps. 311 is in full disguise as chinos-wearing homies with a slight swinger edge—sharp short-sleeved shirts evolved from '40's pachuco wear. Korn was one of the youngest metal-rap acts to score, and its look—scruffy teens with mad dreads on their heads and a spray paint can in their hands—would fit right in at Mook High, Anytown, U.S.A.

Mooks are as diverse as America (even more diverse than America, if you count Swedish rap-rockers Blindside), and their wild, individualistic styles prove that there's nothing whitebread about the mook mindset. The Armenian-American foursome that makes up El Lay's System of a Down kicks a shaved-head, shirt-hanging-open thing that accentuates their menacing dark eyes and Goth tendencies. Rap-metal veterans House of Pain worked a rowdy Irish pride vibe that involved wearing a lot of green. Fortunately for them, it also involved drinking a lot of beer. The multi-culti mix in the Deftones means knee-length dreads for bassist Chi Cheng and Latin gangsta chic for singer Chino Moreno. California bands have a special affinity for cholo style—the fierce facial hair, tank tops, and shades, oversize Dickies, and high-buttoned shirts whose roots are as old as those of the West Coast Latino community. Even the white

73

> "THE DEFTONES' sound is not pretty, so it doesn't communicate happy feelings."
> —Chino Moreno

Early Influences
The Great Wheel of Time Changes Everything

Serj from System of a Down:
Billy Joel, Bee Gees, ABBA

Chino from the Deftones:
The Cure, The Smiths, Depeche Mode

Jonathan Davis of Korn:
Duran Duran and other New Romantic hair bands

All three Beastie Boys:
have seen the Grateful Dead live

CHAMBER

boys in Biohazard look like they're stepping out for the hangover menudo at East L.A.'s La Abeja.

Because rapcore is all about the music, and the music is all about individuality, the look is a moshpit, a free-for-all, a tag-sale riot at Mooks 'R' Us. Princess Superstar, a rare female mook with more balls than all 107 boy bands put together, drops snarky-ass hip-rock while living her Barbie dream in long blond hair and sultry shades. Coal Chamber, another outfit blessed with a member with two X-chromosomes gets Goth in black leather and so much eyeliner even Cher might ask the guys in the group to tone it down. It wouldn't be an exploration of mook style without crowning the kings of freaky-styley, Insane Clown Posse, for turning rapcore into a carny side-show of face paint and prankster attitude. The Posse and the Juggalos who love them blast out-of-the-box style to the next level, where the awesome truth might be coming from a mad clown with a chainsaw.

EMINEM

A. Jay Popoff of **Lit** was arrested in Charlotte, NC, for dropping his pants onstage. He also streaked at House of Blues in Hollywood. Furthermore, he claims to have either written or recorded "My Own Worst Enemy" while naked.

I hurt so bad inside I wish you could see the world through my eyes."
—Korn

KID ROCK

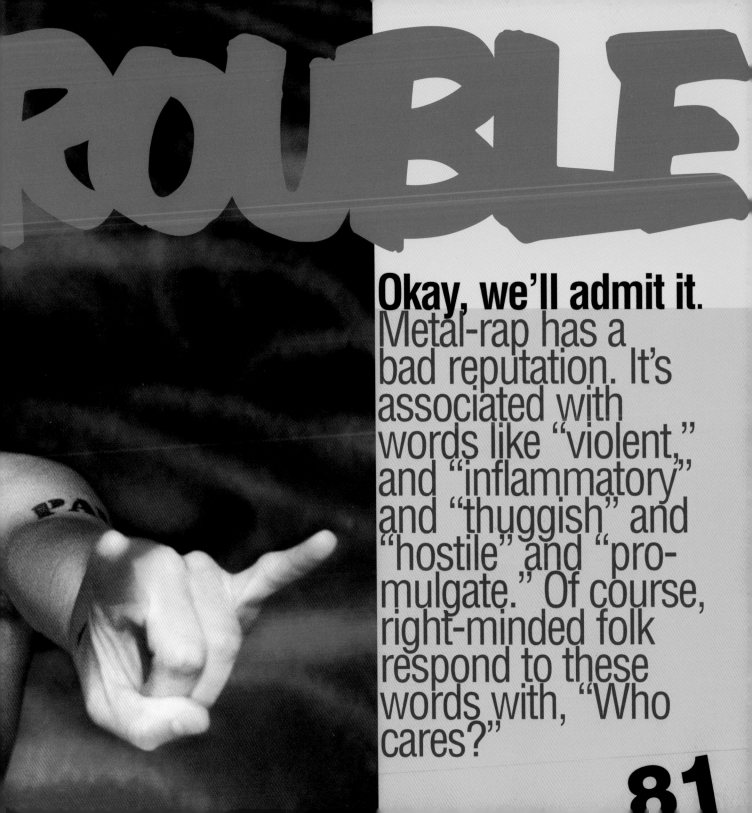

ROUBLE

Okay, we'll admit it. Metal-rap has a bad reputation. It's associated with words like "violent," and "inflammatory" and "thuggish" and "hostile" and "promulgate." Of course, right-minded folk respond to these words with, "Who cares?"

81

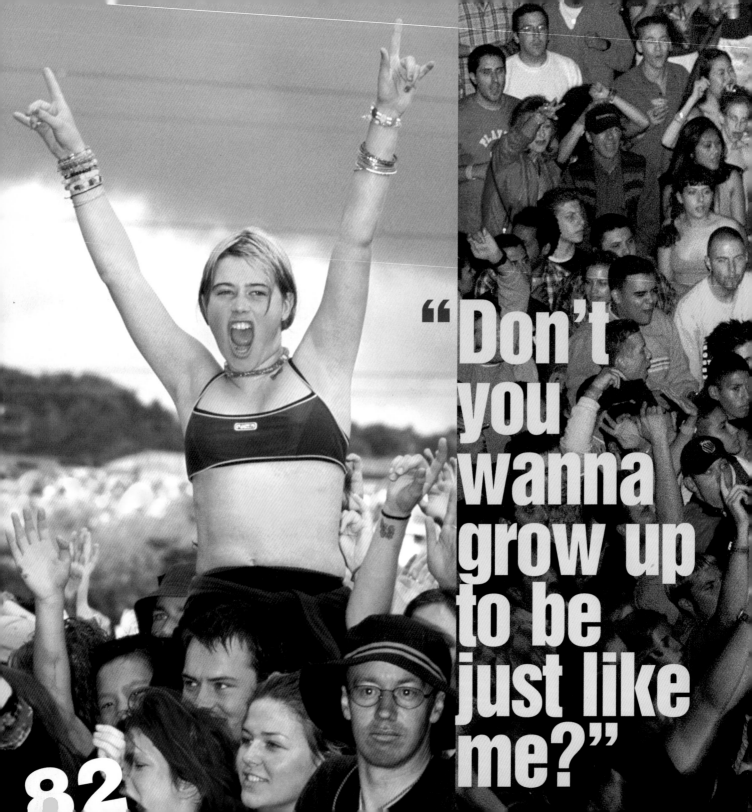

“ **Don't you wanna grow up to be just like me?”**

At an appearance on a San Francisco radio show, DJ Sista Tamu broke a record of *My Name* in half on the air. Later, **Eminem** was menaced by hippies in hippie mecca Haight-Ashbury, but he smacked them up.

("Promulgate" we just ignore until we can look it up.) Then people start using nasty words, like "ban" and "censor," and they start throwing around phrases like "if they try to check in, pretend we don't have any rooms."

Now, you're talking about halting the process of democracy and robbing the fans of freedom of choice and leaving tired touring musicians shivering on the sidewalk and frantically phoning the local Travelodge.

Excuse us for thinking that rock 'n' roll was never about playing nice. It's metal-rap's job to bulldoze boundaries, put them through a wood chipper, burn the pulp, and lick up the ashes. Everyone has a mission on this earth; if someone loses an eye in the process, well, that's rock 'n' roll.

Rapcore made the powers that be berserk from its birth. There wasn't anything dangerous about the music—all music is just music—or even the lyrics; rock lyrics have always been vehicles for fantasy and outlets for our deepest secrets. The trouble with rapcore was that it brought together too many angry young people into what the authorities feared could become an uncontrollable mob.

It used to be easy enough to shut down virtually every hip-hop stadium or club show with a vague explanation about possible violence or overcrowding, so long as the audience was a youthful and powerless segment of the traditionally shafted black population. And metal bands have been hauled into court for decades because some parents blamed everyone but themselves for their screwed-up, depressed, or suicidal kids. As long as the underclass stayed in manageable grouplets, the Man could slice and dice them with ease. But when Ice-T's Body Count used head-banging rock to rap about retaliation against the notoriously trigger-happy LAPD, two huge audiences combined their rage and their voices, and the NRA and police activist groups scrambled to shut Body Count down. The monolithic music industry got into the act once they smelled a drop in profits and refused to release Ice-T's *Home Invasion* album. The revolution was underway.

What pisses off the Man about rapcore? It can be anything. In 1998, a student in Michigan was suspended for wearing a Korn T-shirt. The school's principal proved himself a real pal and a music expert by calling Korn "indecent, vulgar, and obscene." Who knew high-school principals listened to Korn?! That's $16.95 the boys didn't need. The principal was courageous, too—when the band issued a cease-and-desist order, the school backed down.

Bizarre behavior is not specific to rock stars, but they do it with more style than anyone else,

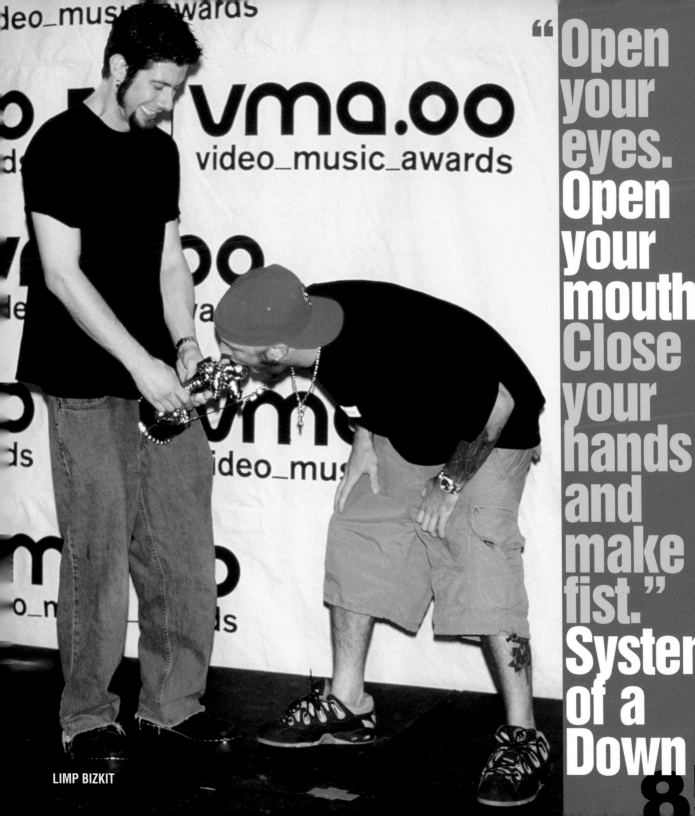

vma.oo
video_music_awards

LIMP BIZKIT

"Open your eyes. Open your mouth. Close your hands and make a fist." System of a Down

85

86

except maybe washed-up aging sexpots who throw hissy fits in airports and smack cops around. When Everlast was the prime mover in House of Pain, he brought a little pain on himself by bouncing into Kennedy Airport with a pistol, unlicensed, unregistered and, to be fair, unloaded. Can you say disoriented, B-level movie star? And as if the 2000 MTV Video Music Awards weren't exciting enough, Tim Commerford of Rage Against the Machine acted out his youthful hijinks by climbing the stage set and rocking back and forth on it while Limp Bizkit tried to make an acceptance speech. That action earned Commerford a charge for disturbing the peace.

As for Bizkit, they got caught in a firestorm that might or might not be of the members' own mak-

RAGE AGAINST THE MACHINE

Violent J and Shaggy 2 Dope turn rap and roll into the theater of the grotesque... or is it the other way around?

88

And Now, A Special Trouble Flashback with Some of Our Favorite Pranksters, Insane Clown Posse

" So I told that old Gypsy woman to stuff it . . . " Cursed, unlucky, or just stupid? Insane Clown Posse foolishly laughs in the face of doom.

On the 1997 ICP tour, Violent J clubs an audience member with a microphone. He is arrested.

What the band was doing when its tour bus ran off the road, we don't want to know. J ends up with a concussion.

Brawl at the waffle house! J and Shaggy Two Dope end up facing disorderly conduct charges. Guys, no one serves real maple syrup anymore; move beyond it.

Violent J, still unable to find his happy place, is seized with a panic attack and can't finish the set. This can be partially explained by the fact that ICP was playing Minnesota at the time.

1999: Let the feuding begin! ICP and Coal Chamber trade barbs—hey, pick on someone your own size. But better times are on the horizon—the boys are offered a slot at Woodstock.

A new century, and Shaggy celebrates by letting his blood-sugar level plummet in the middle of a flu attack and collapses onstage. Maybe the boys could use a foray into something less dangerous than rock & roll, something like . . .

Wrestling! Ooh, sorry, Shaggs, no steel cage is sturdy enough to hold you. One broken nose and one broken cheekbone—that's going to leave a mark.

Who Hates You, Baby? Rapcore's Enemies List

1 The Police
2 The Disney Company
3 Britney Spears
4 The Media
5 The Southern Baptist Convention

KORN

"I was a straight-up thug. We stole tons of car stereos from everywhere and we would sell them to our homies. In between stealing car stereos and sometimes even cars, we would work more fucked-up jobs. Shaggy and his brother John were masters of stealing. They would steal expensive books, jackets, CDs and shit and then take them back to a different store for the loot. Anything. Food, toothpaste, fuckin' ironing boards, fuckin' Chia pets, whatever."
—Violent J

91

92

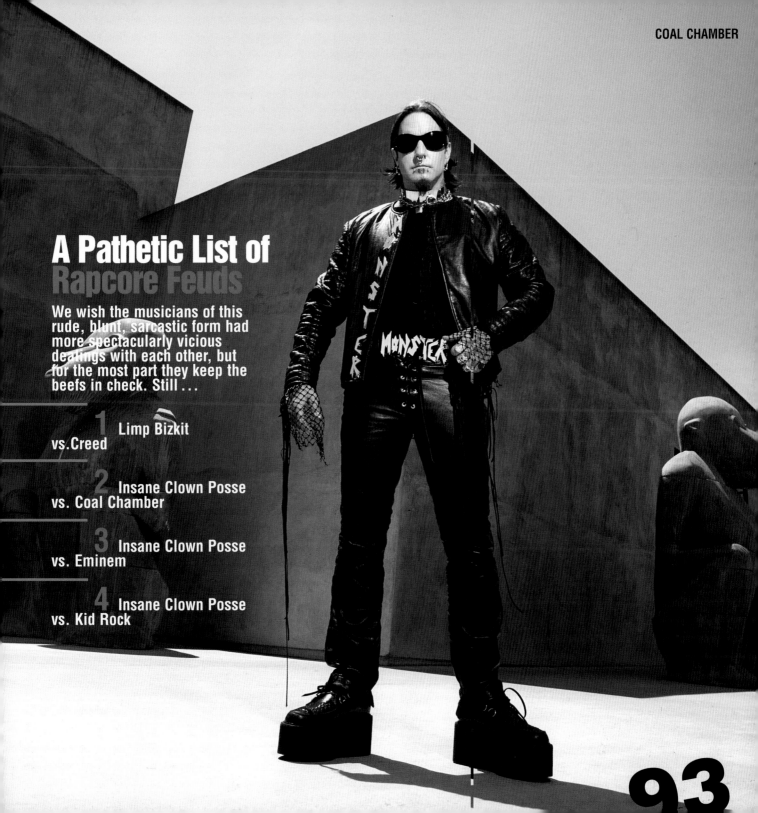

A Pathetic List of
Rapcore Feuds

We wish the musicians of this rude, blunt, sarcastic form had more spectacularly vicious dealings with each other, but for the most part they keep the beefs in check. Still . . .

1 Limp Bizkit
vs. Creed

2 Insane Clown Posse
vs. Coal Chamber

3 Insane Clown Posse
vs. Eminem

4 Insane Clown Posse
vs. Kid Rock

ing. To this day, no one knows exactly what changed Woodstock '99 from a raucous celebration to a bitter firestorm. This much is clear—people got drunk, girls got roughed up, and fires were set. Things got knocked over. From the chaos of the moshpit, maybe it did look like the world was coming to an end and human beings were reverting back to beasthood. But from Bizkit's point of view, the crazed fans, the heat and the screaming probably looked like all its other concerts, only on the biggest, wildest scale. "Break Stuff," kids, is a song. If Fred Durst told you to wear Spandex, is it his fault if you do it?

Rapcore trouble usually doesn't leave a mark. The music's enemies tend to make statements of their own by slapping bands with concert restrictions or fining them for obscenity, whatever that is. When WSUC, SUNY Cortland's college radio station, played Kid Rock's "Yo-Da-Lin in the Valley," the station was fined a staggering $23,750 before a later judgment threw the charge out. Was it the subject matter (oral sex) or the profanity Kid used to describe the subject matter? It doesn't matter, because if Kid wanted massive radio airplay and a mainstream hit from the song, he would have cleaned it up. But he wrote it for the fans. He plays it for the fans. And nobody else has to listen. Mook music is built without compromise.

If MTV wants to put Eminem in heavy rotation, they'll have to bleep out every other *$#?!ing word, because there simply *is* no nice radio-sweet Eminem songs all tidied up and ready to jock for mainstream dollars; hell, ICP is never going to get played anywhere, ever, and so what? In a so-called free society, you don't get to ban everything you don't agree with. And that's something the Man doesn't understand.

94

BEASTIE BOYS

The politically charged So Cal band SYSTEM OF A DOWN, who support Armenian causes and speak eloquently in defense of civic skepticism and cannabis legalization, wrote "KITT" about David Hasselhoff.

95

WIMMEN

On Planet Mook, where testosterone makes up most of the atmosphere.... women still rule. But only the really nasty ones. They have to be able to put up with roiling mosh pits, Show Us Your Tits signs, facial fuzz and body hardware, obscene language and gestures, and decibel levels that could blast a rainforest into a scorched infernal veldt.

If there are any nice girls who are metal-rap fans, we don't want to hear about it. Really bad, super naughty, megasexy chicks are the ultimate mook accessory—

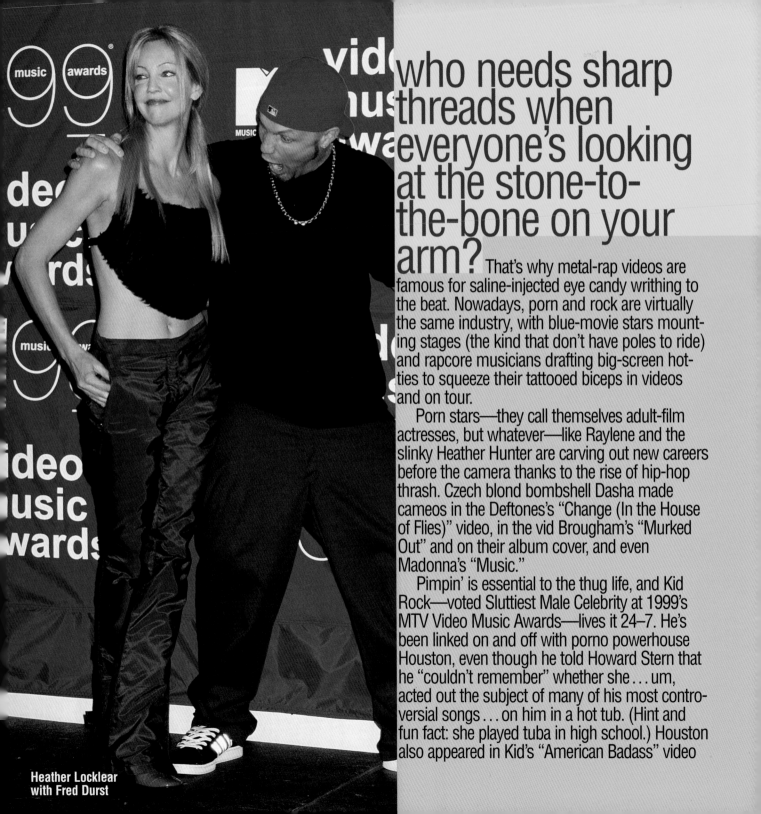

who needs sharp threads when everyone's looking at the stone-to-the-bone on your arm?

That's why metal-rap videos are famous for saline-injected eye candy writhing to the beat. Nowadays, porn and rock are virtually the same industry, with blue-movie stars mounting stages (the kind that don't have poles to ride) and rapcore musicians drafting big-screen hotties to squeeze their tattooed biceps in videos and on tour.

Porn stars—they call themselves adult-film actresses, but whatever—like Raylene and the slinky Heather Hunter are carving out new careers before the camera thanks to the rise of hip-hop thrash. Czech blond bombshell Dasha made cameos in the Deftones's "Change (In the House of Flies)" video, in the vid Brougham's "Murked Out" and on their album cover, and even Madonna's "Music."

Pimpin' is essential to the thug life, and Kid Rock—voted Sluttiest Male Celebrity at 1999's MTV Video Music Awards—lives it 24–7. He's been linked on and off with porno powerhouse Houston, even though he told Howard Stern that he "couldn't remember" whether she . . . um, acted out the subject of many of his most controversial songs . . . on him in a hot tub. (Hint and fun fact: she played tuba in high school.) Houston also appeared in Kid's "American Badass" video

Heather Locklear with Fred Durst

KID ROCK with James King

How To Be A Pimp

1 Surround yourself with really hot babes.

2 Hats—big; limos—big; jewelry—big.

3 The good news: Pimps can be fat. It's not your body earning the cheddar.

4 Pimpin' often requires wearing fur, but under no circumstances should it be called "fun fur."

5 Remember the law of inverse ho-response: you can either treat 'em to silk wraps and stiletto heels OR you can push 'em around and show them who's boss. Do not try to show a girl armed with a silk wrap and stiletto heels who's boss.

99

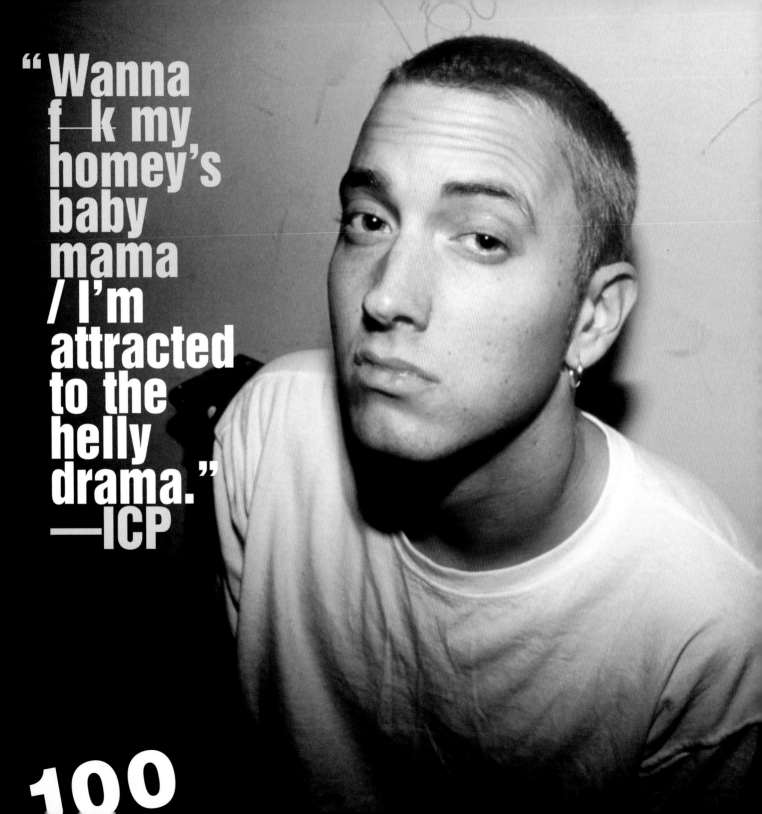

"Wanna f—k my homey's baby mama / I'm attracted to the helly drama."
—ICP

100

EMINEM

along with other pornettes, and she posed for an album cover along with Claudia Chase and Coral Sands.

Kid Rock snaps his weedy white fingers, and all the biggest names in the XXX-world come running: Midori, little sister of '80s dance diva Jody Watley, is also a musician, with the lap-dance anthem "5-10-15-20"; exotic Kobe Tai; and incendiary Jenna Jameson, who was actually banned by the Academy of Recording Arts and Sciences from performing with Rock at the 2000 Grammys. It was an act of sheer hypocrisy—the Academy deemed the porn queen too much of a dirty bird for their fine, family-oriented awards show just because Jameson is a recognizable adult-film "name." But they did allow him to decorate the stage with lesser-known porn princesses, so whatevuh. On top of linking up with bodacious bodies who do the hardcore thing, Kid Rock has put in his time with the very busy Carmen Electra. (This might be in the standard mook record contract. See under: Durst, Fred and Real B.)

But lately Kid's cleaned up his private act, even if the public one is still a celebration of shit-kicking lowlife. He's been stepping out with stick-figure fashion model James King, who'll only take off her clothes if someone with a name like Meisel is behind the lens. Many mooks have normal girlfriends and even wives, presumably extremely strong women who can withstand the hazards of road life and being attached to a scruffy guy in baggy clothes who every female with in a 10-mile radius wants to get with. Coal Chamber's singer Dez actually left the band just as its demonic nitro-metal started to ignite the Los Angeles club scene, because his music was tearing his marriage apart. He wised up—or

HOW TO PLEASE A MOOK

Shut up. Bring him another beer. Don't deconstruct the lyrics to his new song, even if you suspect it's about you. Get the implants. Shake that thang. Shut UP.

Flea from RED HOT CHILI PEPPERS: So what if she's fiberglass? You think Dave Matthews gets chicks this hot?

103

Are You a Metal-Rap Ho? Take Our Quiz!

You want a piercing. Do you go for
    a) another set in your earlobes. It's so naughty!
    b) maybe a nose stud for evening.
    c) a new double-ball barbell. This time real silver. Intimate chafing is no joke.

Your fan letters begin
    a) Dreamiest N'Sync, I don't know which one of you is the cutest...
    b) Mr. Hasselfhoff, You are a great singer and actor...
    c) Dear Pam Anderson, After watching your video, my guy and I made this bet...

Do you smoke?
    a) Never!
    b) Maybe one after dinner or at a nightclub.
    c) Only menthols 'cause no one wants to bum 'em off you. Plus, they're minty fresh.

What's your attitude toward his ex-girlfriend?
    a) If he's with me now, he's over her.
    b) I used to get jealous, but I'm over it.
    c) For a while she had a nasty bruise, but she put a lot of blusher over it. Broke my fingernail, too.

When did fringed halter tops come back in style?
    a) What kind of trampy female would wear a fringed halter top?
    b) Golly, that would be, like, 1999?
    c) Come back???

"Do you think I'm a
—Kittie

whore?"

107

maybe the little woman did—because she walked out and Dez renewed his vows with his first love, making ears bleed and spreading the dark gospel.

Coal Chamber is the rare rapcore outfit that includes a curvilicious actual woman-type creature, spooky wraithlike bassist Rayna. But mookhood isn't about being a guy, it's about responding to the mainstream music industry, to sheeplike fans who'll worship every well-groomed robot on MTV, to slick beats and fake fronting, with a big fat middle-finger wave and a wiggling moon. There's only one genuine metal-rap superstar princess—that would be Princess Superstar—and if she's not actually a man, everyone's too afraid to tell her. But plenty of hard chicks are putting over mook style without the sound—like the old-school speedmetal queens Kittie.

Mostly, though, wimmen exist in mookland to cause woman trouble, and when metal-rap bands write songs about girls, they're not sitting in a sunny meadow remembering her sweet touch on his trembling shoulder. These ladies will take your money, bone on your homies, refuse to help move your amps, and get in your face screaming if you object to any of these actions. (They tend to roll their necks around when they're screaming, and watch out for the nails, 'cause that silk wrap can take an eye out.) You got a problem with that? Get a job in retail. There isn't a single metal-rap star who'll front that he didn't get into music to score honey. So, you know, be careful what you wish for.

Don't lie, Fred. You know you want her.

Britney

110

"Hell, I'd like to be the first really famous white girl rapper. But I can tell you right now ...it's not gonna be me 'cause I'm too weird."

Satan loves you!

666

FAILED

FAILED

YOU'VE BEEN TRICKED

P

112

Rock 'n' roll is a political form. Strip music of everything but its capacity to harmlessly entertain the maximum number of people in a pleasant, inoffensive way, and you've got something that can no longer be called music, except in the most general, most Wayne Newton sense. Guitar chords and drumbeats are just noise without the stuff that makes rock rock—a balls-out attitude, an aggressive stance, and a willingness to mix it up when the big issues come calling.

114

Metal-rap's very existence is a political statement.

While it originally brought together two groups of outcast fans, as it developed, the anarchic energy of the sound began to attract people of various races, classes and religions without question or judgment. No other musical form can boast of having stars from such a wide range of backgrounds or points of view.

There are hyphenate-Americans all over rap-core—African-, Irish-, Armenian-, Asian-, and Latino-Americans. Often, a band member's ethnicity finds its way into the music, the group's pride and eclecticism on public display. As rap-core spreads its tentacles of influence around the globe, there are even bands with the same attitude popping up in other countries, including the Scandinavian-non-American punk-rap outfit Blindside, from Stockholm.

Blindside also is one of the strongest and most popular alternative CCM groups—Contemporary Christian Music hard-rockers with a taste for the preaching aggression of hip-hop who express their Christian faith through their music. P.O.D. (Payable On Death) got in the faith-and-head-banging game almost a decade ago, in 1992, when they hit on the band name that not only has a hardcore edge but a message about Judgment Day. Their lyrics are heavily disguised by the distorted metal, and hip-hop, and Latin influences that fuel the music.

Omaha, Nebraska's 311 has been putting over positive metal-rap since 1990; while not a

115

116

BLINDSIDE

Christian rock outfit, the five "friends for life" shared a taste for rowdy rock and for uplifting lyrical messages.

Some bands take political stances just by trying to have a good time. Orange County's Kottonmouth Kings got that dry-tongue feeling by being major weed fans, at least in song and story. (We're not trying to get anyone arrested here.) Giving its albums titles like *Royal Highness*, *Hidden Stash*, and the EP *Stoners Reeking Havoc*, the psychedelic hip-hop punk rockers, as they call themselves, have never hidden their, uh,

117

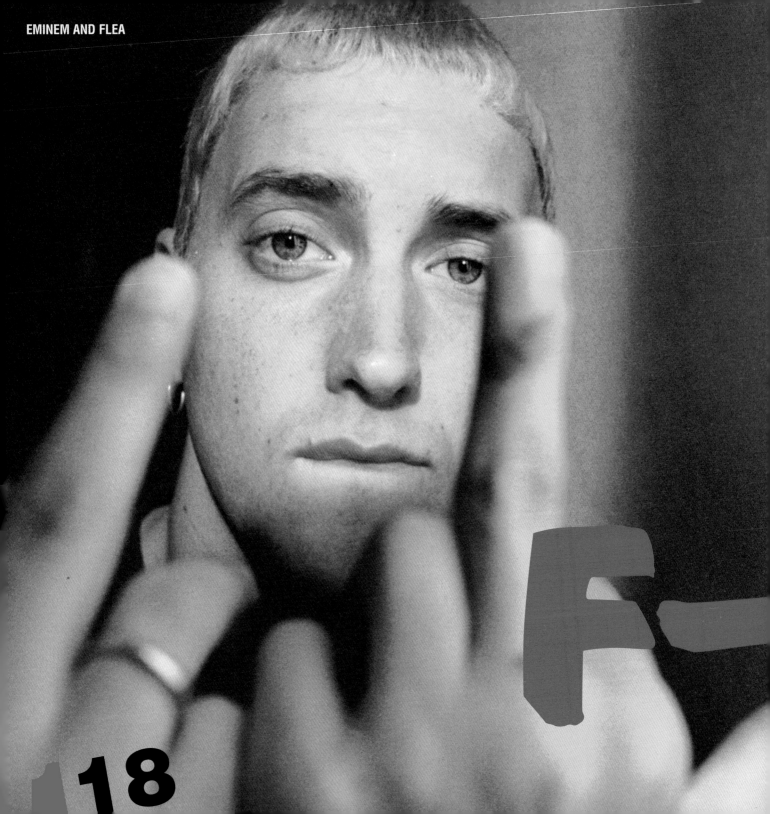

18

you

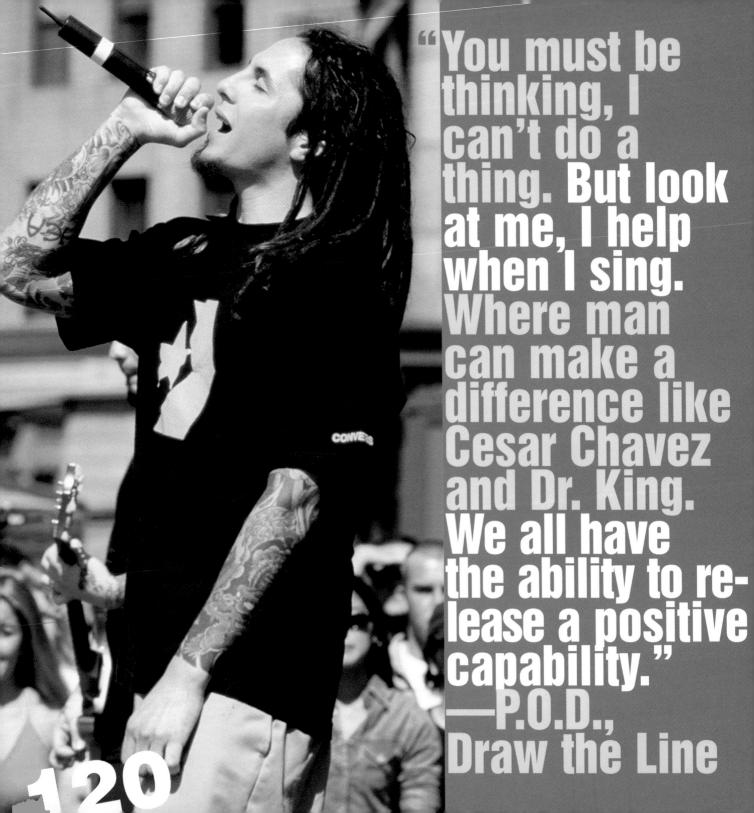

"You must be thinking, I can't do a thing. But look at me, I help when I sing. Where man can make a difference like Cesar Chavez and Dr. King. We all have the ability to release a positive capability."
—P.O.D., Draw the Line

121

blunt passion. Having a taste for a method of relaxation outside the mainstream is one of Kottonmouth's prime motivators for their angry, questioning, anti-government lyrics. Members of Cypress Hill were the first and most outspoken weed advocates; they performed in front of a huge cannabis banner and fired up onstage, their beats were as baked as their brains, and they never backed down from campaigning for herbal legalization.

In 1991, the world that Anthrax came from—the world of mouth-breathing, hair-flailing metal—wasn't known for its controversial stances. But Anthrax's fascination with hip-hop led to a choice in partners that pulled no punches. When it teamed up with Public Enemy for "Bring Tha Noize," Anthrax was making a statement. P.E. was the most muckraking, establishment-taunting black militant group in the world, and this collaboration was a testament not just to the music's power but to the political force of crossing borders and opening new ones.

Being on the outside forces people to think for themselves, and if they can become a success without any help from the established structure, everyone's gonna hear about it. That's why hip-hop artists throughout history have built anti-establishment boasts into their titles, lyrics, and label names. It's also why O.G. hip-hop stars like Ice-T deliberately set out to annoy censors and Tipper Gores—we'd expect no less from the man who invented metal-rap. New York City's Princess Superstar has been screwing with music-industry traditions for years, founding an independent record label in 1996 that she called A Big Rich Major Label and naming her album CEO. Just to prove that she ain't half-stepping, after she began to achieve international recognition on the

RAGE AGAINST THE MACHINE

123

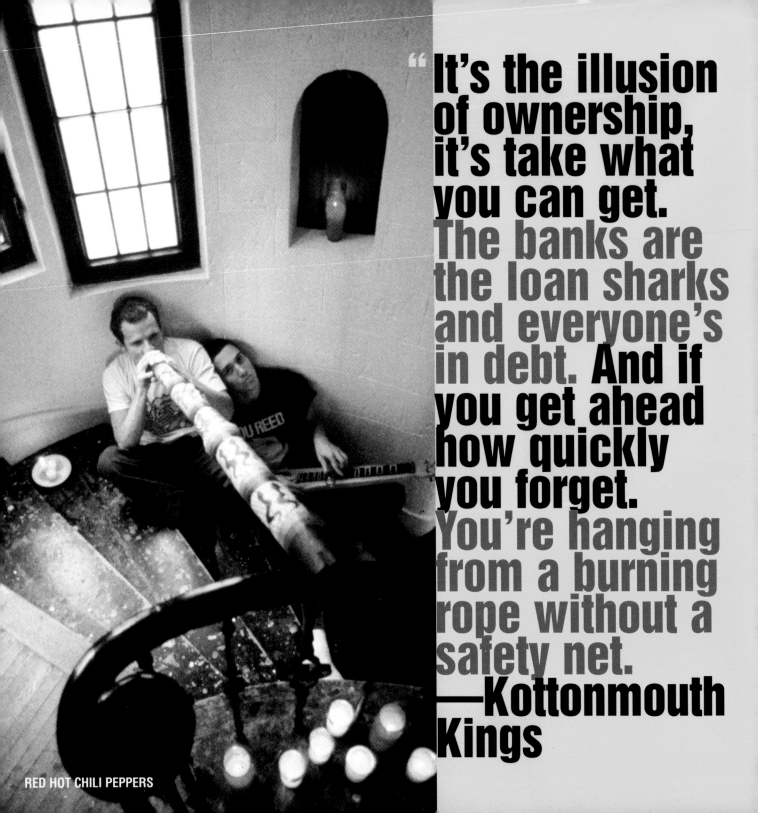

> "It's the illusion of ownership, it's take what you can get. The banks are the loan sharks and everyone's in debt. And if you get ahead how quickly you forget. You're hanging from a burning rope without a safety net.
> —Kottonmouth Kings

RED HOT CHILI PEPPERS

125

strength of her Hostile Takeover Tour '98, a month-and-a-half juggernaut through North America, Princess renamed the label Corrupt Conglomerate.

But the most outspoken musicans are the ones who take stands on controversial issues. It's activists, anarchists, and firebrands who keep the dialogue free and open in what's supposed to be a free and open society... unless you say something the folks in charge don't want to hear. Limp Bizkit's Fred Durst's advocacy of online music trading in general and Napster in particular earned him the enmity, ironically, of some of Bizkit's musical idols, including Napster Enemy #1, Metallica. But Durst has always maintained that his music is for the kids, and that the more access the more people have to Bizkit's sound, the better the world will be. And who says that self-sacrifice never pays? Napster sponsored Bizkit on a free summer 2000 tour.

No discussion of hardcore politics would be complete without props to the most outspoken rock 'n' roll militants on the scene. Rage Against the Machine brought fiery polemics back into music, which hadn't seen such fierce leftist protest rock since the '60s. But there's nothing hippie about Rage, which combined the band's agile musicianship with Zack de la Rocha's provocative sloganeering and an incendiary onstage energy. Kids out for a mere rockin' good time who ran headfirst into Rage found themselves pulled into a whirlwind of issue-oriented, thought-provoking, establishment-questioning, rap-metal that made fans think as hard as it made them rock.

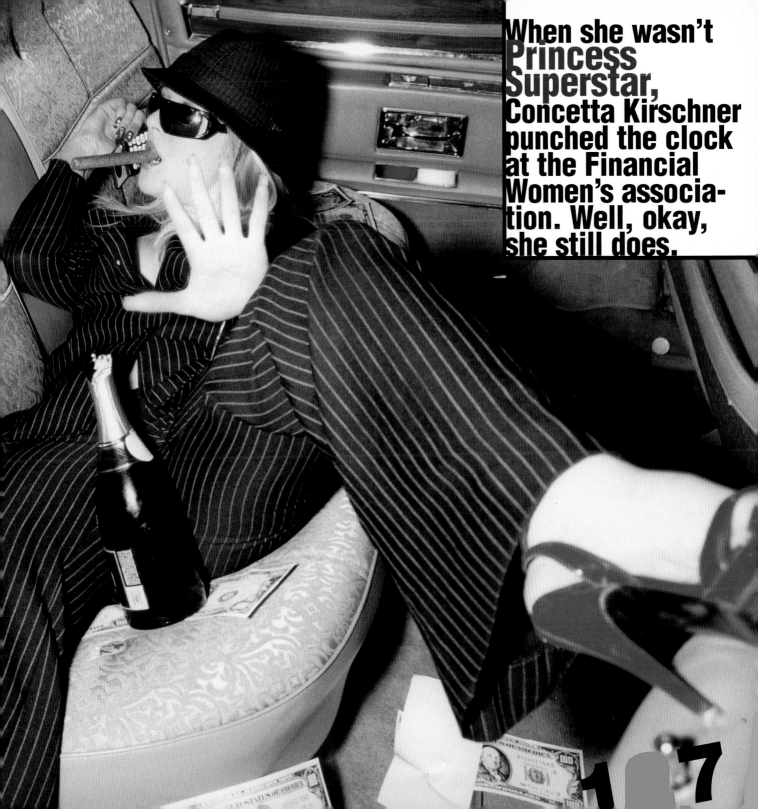

When she wasn't **Princess Superstar**, Concetta Kirschner punched the clock at the Financial Women's association. Well, okay, she still does.

127

782.4216 Berger, Arion.
49
Ber   Hardcore rap.

DATE			
10-23-02			